W9-DEV-383

DATE DUE			

☆

What
Saves Us

☆

What Saves Us

Poems by
Bruce Weigl

TriQuarterly Books
Northwestern University

Acknowledgements

I am grateful to the editors for permission to reprint poems that first appeared in the following publications: *American Poetry Review*: "The Impossible," "The Third Person," "They Name Heaven," "The Husband," "Anna's Grace," "The Biography of Fatty's Bar and Grille," "Blues in the Afterworld," "Shelter," "For the Luminous Woman in the Trees," "The Forms of Eleventh Avenue" and "Why We Are Forgiven." *Christian Science Monitor*: "The Unattainable Body of Light." *Colorado Review*: "What Saves Us." *Indiana Review*: "On the Dictatorship of the Proletariat." *Ironwood*: "Winter Meditation, 1970." *Kenyon Review*: "The Confusion of Planes You Must Wander in Sleep." *Mānoa*: "Why Nothing Changes for Miss Ngo Thi Thanh." *Missouri Review*: "The Black Hose." *New England Review*: "The Loop." *Ohio Review*: "Meditation at Pearl Street," "The Hand That Takes" (in a radically different form) and "Autumn in the New Town." *Open Places*: "The Offices of Loss." *Quarry West*: "May." *Quarterly West*: "Temptation" and "Meditation" (as "Meditation at Buckroe Beach"). *Southern Review*: "Her Life Runs Like a Red Silk Flag" and "Elegy for the Swans at Grace Pond." *Tar River Poetry*: "The Years Without Understanding." *TriQuarterly*: "This Man," "In the Days Before Insurrection," "In the House of Immigrants," "In the Autumn Village," "April," "Amigo del Corazón," "Blues at the Equinox" and "Breakdown." *Western Humanities Review*: "The Sky in Daduza Township."

"The Black Hose," "What Saves Us," "Anna's Grace," "The Confusion of Planes We Must Wander in Sleep," "Meditation at Pearl Street" and "They Name Heaven" also appeared in *New American Poets of the Nineties* (David Godine, 1992).

Thanks to the National Endowment for the Arts for a pre-1989 grant which allowed time and support to complete this manuscript without threat of censorship. And special thanks to Andrew Weigl for his criticism and his inspiration.

Books by Bruce Weigl

Poetry

Executioner (1976)
Like a Sackful of Old Quarrels (1977)
A Romance (1979)
The Monkey Wars (1984)
Song of Napalm (1988)

Criticism

The Giver of Morning: On Dave Smith (1983)
The Imagination as Glory: The Poetry of James Dickey
    (with T. R. Hummer) (1984)
The Phenomenology of Spirit and Self: On the Poetry of
    Charles Simic (1992)

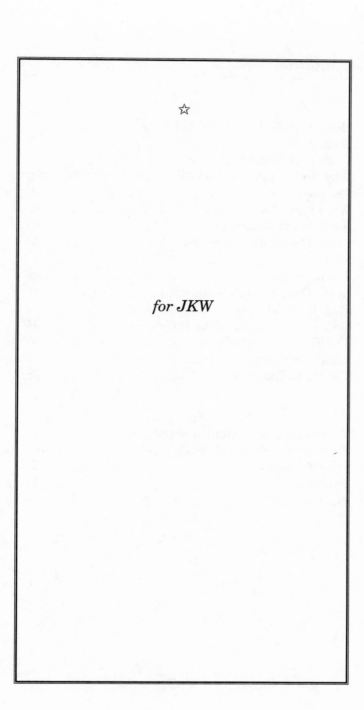

☆

for JKW

Contents

I

The song was wordless
The singing will never be done

Siegfried Sassoon

Her Life Runs
Like a Red Silk Flag

Because this evening Miss Hoang Yen
sat down with me in the small
tiled room of her family house
I am unable to sleep.
We shared a glass of cold and sweet water.
On a blue plate her mother brought us
cake and smiled her betel black teeth at me
but I did not feel strange in the house
my country had tried to bomb into dust.
In English thick and dazed as blood
she told me how she watched our planes
cross her childhood's sky,
all the children of Hanoi
carried in darkness to mountain hamlets, Nixon's
Christmas bombing. She let me hold her hand,
her shy unmoving fingers, and told me
how afraid she was those days and how this fear
had dug inside her like a worm and lives
inside her still, won't die or go away.
And because she's stronger, she comforted me,
said I'm not to blame,
the million sorrows alive in her gaze.
With the dead we share no common rooms.
With the frightened we can't think straight;
no words can bring the burning city back.
Outside on Hung Dao Street
I tried to say goodbye and held her hand
too long so she looked back through traffic
towards her house and with her eyes
she told me I should leave.

All night I ached for her and for myself
and nothing I could think or pray
would make it stop. Some birds sang morning
home across the lake. In small reed boats
the lotus gatherers sailed out
among their resuming white blossoms.

Hanoi, 1990

Breakdown

With sleep that is barely under the surface
it begins, a twisting sleep as if a wire
were inside you and tried at night
to straighten your body.
Or it's like a twitch
through the nerves as you sleep
so you tear the sheets from the bed
to try and stop the spine from pounding.
A lousy worthless
sleep of strangers with guns,
children trapped in an alley,
teenage soldiers glancing back
over their shoulders
the moment before
they squeeze the trigger.

I am going to stay here as long as I can.
I am going to sit in this garden as if nothing has happened
and let these bruised azaleas have their way.

Winter Meditation, 1970

After the war, after the broken
marriage and failed life,
after the too many jobs,
the too many doctors, so sure
of their enchantments,
after the pills, the diving naked
through the window, after the pills,
their long drowning into nothing,
after the other woman,
the thousand years of grief
in her veins, after the loss,
the broken friends, the deaths
all around us like flies,
we are on the earth
and we have somehow come together
my mother, father
descended to the city where I hide,
to make them believe I'm not a ghost
but here somehow,
among the books and strangers,
the woman's clothes hung
indecently over the mirror,
among the prayers we surrender to no one,
somehow here, with a life,
and my father touches my arm
as if to feel the blood
the way you feel the corpse
when the family has departed
in the black limousine,
and my mother kisses me,

all but an illusive breath
of longing gone,
or no longer for me, that love.

Why Nothing Changes for Miss Ngo Thi Thanh

December in Hanoi
is gray and wet and cold
but in the still dark morning
after tea and rice
she rides her bike through
waking streets, past fallen
temples, to the grim offices
of the War Crimes Commission
where she sorts through pictures
that tell a wordless, armless
story of their own.
But in her mind there are suspicions
and she imagines rooms
with great light in them,
she imagines time enough
to drift away, back
to the Perfume river and her lost
boy's heart. But grinding along
beneath her feet is a country,
a turtle on which her world
is balanced, and over space
vast as these lost lives
she must move with such care
it is all she can do to keep
from falling into the night
these dead inhabit
because they can't go home.
And against winter, against
history, she puts a little lipstick on,

some rouge, she ties a colored
scarf around her black hair.

Hanoi, 1985

The Loop

Blue unwelcome jays barge through trees in the flyway,
God of the great nothing hovering over us.
So long I've wanted the woman of the green year,
in my thighs and in my gut, evening sheen of sweat

on her body on the borrowed bed, summer tearing
apart from the inside, I rolled her nipple
between my lips like a bullet and from a bad
and green dream I was delivered to her forgiving hips.

But certain spirits still inhabit me.
Certain strangers have in their eyes a river on which
you may sail back to the killing ground. I fell back
into her eyes, her body like smoke, the cords of light

that connect us to the world pulsing and
cracking. Some boys fell before me in heaps, their arms
and legs flailing ridiculously through the smoke
and flash. I remember that. I remember

the smell of the Vietnamese woman's hair
on the crowded train as we slowed for the last curve
before home. I remember a necklace of human ears,
everything, in sunlight, I can't stop seeing.

What Saves Us

We are wrapped around each other
in the back of my father's car parked
in the empty lot of the high school
of our failures, sweat on her neck
like oil. The next morning I would leave
for the war and I thought I had something
coming for that, I thought to myself
that I would not die never having
been inside her body. I lifted
her skirt above her waist like an umbrella
blown inside out by the storm. I pulled
her cotton panties up as high
as she could stand. I was on fire. Heaven
was in sight. We were drowning
on our tongues and I tried
to tear my pants off when she stopped
so suddenly we were surrounded
only by my shuddering
and by the school bells
grinding in the empty halls.
She reached to find something,
a silver crucifix on a silver chain,
the tiny savior's head
hanging, and stakes through his hands and his feet.
She put it around my neck and held me
so long my heart's black wings were calmed.
We are not always right
about what we think will save us.
I thought that dragging the angel down that night
would save me, but I carried the crucifix in my pocket

and rubbed it on my face and lips
nights the rockets roared in.
People die sometimes so near you,
you feel them struggling to cross over,
the deep untangling, of one body from another.

Blues in the Afterworld

I remember a wild apple tree
alone in a field where deer had lain
and made a bed in the long leaves of grass
where I slept with a gun
in my hands
and woke in rain
misting on the leaves
and on the hard apple's redness
abandoned to the rattling branches.
I have to say
I put that gun down
and opened my pants
and touched myself.
The light made me do it,
the loneliness,
and brother crow said something
through the distant, broken trees
that sounded like a warning
and in a wild moment
outside myself
I was trapped in a room of flowers,
their smell too much to bear
like it must be for the dead.
Then the room was a boat
on which I sailed
into the hush of a green jungle.
Out of time I was jangled,
out of space
but then just as quickly
delivered back to the empty field,

to the bed deer had made
under red apples,
the world light now in some places
and in some places dark.

In the House of Immigrants

After milk, the kittens spill out of their box,
weary mother cat snapping at them,
too young for so many babies. In the bedroom
the boy bows his cello painfully
down the hall, Mozart. He loves his practice
more than ball with the boys who call him
through the summer's open window. The grandfather
smokes, reads his Hungarian newspaper
moving his lips. The mother cooks
some nice chicken with garlic, some boiled
potatoes, and our children run in and out
of the house as if there were not enough time
to live because there isn't, the solstice sun
already gone below the oaks looming over us,
and I argue with the father.

                          He loves our country
no matter what, he says. There must
be sacrifices, our voices beginning to rise
above the cello, above the children,
above the kitchen noise until everyone freezes,
stares at us fearfully and with disappointment.
We've come too far to stop. I'm not
interested in details he says, only
the principle is important, his hands shaking
between us and a wronged light cast down
on his face until the mother steps
from the kitchen and tells us with her eyes to stop.
She shakes her finger at her husband and says
his name, stressing the syllables the way a mother

calls her child home across the dark
neighborhood and then she turns to me.
I was only a child she says.
They lined you up without a word
and shot you like a dog.
I won't listen to Russian music.
I don't care if you say it is beautiful.
I won't read Russian books.
I don't care what you say.
They buried people in the school yard where I played.

Shelter

I need cover tonight.
I need shelter from the wings
who beat my head into memory
where my sister sleeps
in the small upstairs bedroom
among the crucifixes and dried palm leaves,
among the lavender smell
of our grandmother's Sunday black silk dress
in her house where we've come as a family
after church,
the brothers from Belgrade
and the wives from across the river
which is called the river of blood.

In the crowded kitchen,
below my sleeping sister,
a beautiful dandelion salad
waits like a bouquet
with blood sausage on a plate
and black bread and dark wine,
and the aunts and uncles
and their children in their orbits,
and the language thick on my tongue
when I try to say the words
because the air is suddenly wronged.
My grandfather swears too loud.
His brothers only laugh.
The women shush them all, Eat,
eat they say across the room
but something's cut too deep this time

so the children are pushed
with grace towards the porch and backyard,
and from behind the tree
of drunken plums
I watch my grandfather
wave his pistol in the air
and his brothers reach for it
and the shot explode
through the low ceiling
and the bedroom floor
where my sister sleeps
and lives on.
I need shelter tonight.
I need the sleeping hands
to waken once again.

Temptation

Either in the hotel D'Lido in Managua,
that faddish fifties bar in the garden
and all the hot water the people could not have
splashing extravagantly down your body
into the painted tile drain; or in
the bathhouse in Masaya, anonymous
artillery booming dully in the distance,
and the manliness, at the same time,
let down and untangled like hair,
all of us wrapped like mummies in towels,
speaking a simple Spanish to each other
through the heavy air, our faces visible
only vaguely through the steam. Or in Hanoi,
Christmas eighty-five, Russians
mill around the lobby,
dreaming their warm water port,
their eager interpreters
covering their mouths when they laugh,
and among them, the woman in the flowered *ao dais*
who called to you across the room with her eyes,
across the impossibility
as if imagining your white skin. Or in a cool
bed in Tay Ninh, where you slept with men
across the sheet's white field
through the burning afternoon,
the narrow highway of red dust,
the war-wasted plantations behind you
as you tried to match your breath with theirs
as if to bring them close. Or Lord,
in a dark unthinkable room in Bangkok

where in fever you dreamed that a bad cell,
a swirling red planet out of control
tried to kill the other holy cells
and take your body,
someone's lonely buddha
praying through an open window,
across the alley, across the marketplace,
waves of prayer.

In the Days
Before Insurrection

Lies spread against the people as they sleep.
Dogs bicker all morning through their fences,
reactionaries, they bark and snarl at each other,
at wind kicking dirt in their faces
which wear something like human longing,
at boats in the harbor, calling as if to the lost.

Penned up like this the people and their dogs
pace off their world until there's a path worn,
a boundary within which you may feel
safe from the long knives who speak,
in sleep, to the throat. Men plot.
Men touch themselves and gas the truck in moonlight.
Men feel the weapons to make the shape
of their hands pulling the trigger.
Men draw scarves over their mouths,
their breath makes a wet hole. Dogs howl.
Angels abandon their earthly corners
and this is where you stop believing:

many in darkness are taken away.
You're at home dozing or reading magazines
and many are driven to the low hill beyond the plaza.
You're watching your children play.
You're breathing easier and more are taken.
Fists beat through the doors
of rooms where children are afraid to cry out.
Where the powder burns, the sheet is black then red.
Where the crucifix bleeds, words are dirt
stuffed in the mouths of the chosen.

They Name Heaven

I saw the moon over Plaza España
but it's not my moon
because of what this pale one has seen
pass in dark cells at the hands
of crazy rich men,
murder on their lips like salt.
Not the moon my little boy will see tonight
safe in the place of the great Republic,
near enough his mother
so he may find her even in his sleep.
Not the clean moon he calls to,
this one rises over Cuesta del Plomo
where the bones have already grown
back into the earth
until there is nothing
but the disappeared.
The moon who will no longer
let us understand each other.
How in darkness they came for you.
How in moonlight you passed through the city,
your hands bound,
your shirt ripped over your face.
How you must have known you would die
only wondered how long it would take,
what parts of the body they would relish
with their sticks and long knives,
those who make pacts under the moon,
who wash the blood away with rum,
and return to their sleeping families
to lift the acquiescent

nightgowns of their wives,
their drunken lips
fumbling upwards, always
upwards to the moons of flesh
they name heaven.

On the Dictatorship of the Proletariat

At a party of the young Sandinistas in Managua,
neighborhood where the Somocistas had lived
and idled their long cars,
all the pretty people dance the salsa
and toast the liberation with fine rum.

Two winding miles down the hill
a barrio of tin-roofed shacks
spreads itself out like a sickness.
On dirt floors the people keep house,
they fetch their water in buckets,

through a field of garbage they pick like gulls
for a slice of fruit or scrap of meat.
A boy had grabbed my hand down there
and led me through the mud and morning
light, proud about something he wanted me to see,

a sewer being dug but now abandoned.
He jumped down into that ordinary hole
and waved his arms
like it was his grave he'd just defeated,
or like it was a monument,
because not having to shit
in the tall grass means something.

The Sky in Daduza Township

Like a green turtle on the dusty highway
a small car is on its back, only burning,
black smoke curdling in plumes,
in great billows against the white sky
that opens itself to some terror.
A man calls to someone out of frame.
He cradles the bloodied hands of his friend
whose eyes are half-closed as if about to sleep
only they look down at what's left of his hands
that have been shot or smashed
with something heavy
the vigilantes carried
through the bent-up stalks
of surrounding fields,
come and gone like a storm.
Another man spreads his arms
as if welcoming someone home
from a long journey
except his eyes say that no one comes.
Around him black smoke curdles,
huge blossoms of smoke you feel
you could pluck from the air,
and around the last man too,
who holds a child over his head
like a sack of something he's lifted
from a truck and is about to throw into a pile
of more sacks and in the air
so many angels you can't breathe,
their wings in your face like fingers,
like a white-capped river of voices
the wind spits when whatever spirits survive
are called to cross over,
the howling blows rained down, rained down.

Amigo del Corazón

In a café in barrio Las Américas,
a lovely dark man has become my friend
drinking so much beer
we fall into each other's arms
in the shadows of palms
while his daughter,
the flower named Anna Ester,
sips her juice through a straw
and can't help not sway to a salsa
coming in from someone's lonely radio.
Flower of the night garden,
her eyes are on her father as he speaks,
her face open to him
because a radiance is still possible.

He pulls his pants leg up
for me to see the scar of the wound
where shrapnel burnt a white
crescent moon into his brown skin.
We live mostly in silence he says,
in houses smaller than the shape
he draws with his finger
in the air around this room.

We have not done well enough he says,
not even love can save you from certain
memories, the beer spilling at his lips
until he's quiet, and the music gone,
and the heart quiet too in its time
so we can hear the nightbird

sing what sounds like loss
into the dark barrio
and sing again,
but no song returns
and I feel myself
lift away from the ghosts he recalls
who crowd around to sing
their own grind of troop trucks
and the rattle of weapons
in the houses of those
who will not let the terror return.
He reaches for my hand to pull me back.
He touches his heart
and then he touches my heart, too.

The Hand That Takes

Sometimes I think it's God I want,
that I need the holy spirit
as if the lost years,
the sins of my body and hands
could be forgiven.
The days not unlike a song
twist in my head
and something old and evil
clings like a bad smell
and a hand
wants to take and take.
Rain washes the blood
until the blood seeps away
but leaves a ruby
shadow on the ground.
Wings cut.
There was fire
in her eyes
so we didn't touch.
I wanted her silk
on my cock,
her lips, her nipples,
but soldiers ran wild
through Tet's streets
and spotlights
swung in arcs from jeeps.
You cannot hide
from what eats you.
She still calls me
from the room in an alley
where the boy I was

undressed
but kept one hand
on the black weapon
all through the night
of wronged love,
the worthless money
spread out on the bed
like a fan.
Yet tonight
through the years
I hear my woman speak
to our little boy
and the thousands
of holes in my brain
and their screaming
can't drown what sounds
like song to make him sleep,
like promises that are lies,
kisses that will not come
as he believes
forever to his lips.
I have grown up inside
a thing that I can't name.
I spoke with angels once.
Through their slipless
pastel dresses
I traced that ancient silhouette.
I imagined what I could do
to their bodies
but sharp wings
cut through their clothes
and their claws like a dog's
ripped a hole in the sky.
What used to save me
was my child's voice
singing at night in his bed
songs he'd learned at school
or the pills that gave me sleep

or the light come up
on rain-misted trees.
I have loved war.
I have loved the nights
of dragons and opium,
the wind from the river
in the angel's hair,
her skin like silk
on the balcony of the dead
in the blood
of my breaking free
because I did not die
with those who rose
beyond the green,
drowning like visions.
And after that dangerous love
no woman could save me
from the meaning of things.
I wanted to lie down with her
as if nothing had happened
and the air could be breathed
and the atoms of light
did not explode
in our faces like flares.
I heard a hallelujah
through the wind.
I heard a child's scream
and the rockets
crash through bamboo.
From the mother's legs
we are dropped into fire.
There is not even time
for the moon to turn away,
or the words to be said
and then mean nothing,
or the fear to make men
not kiss the dead.

II

Far off, Oh keep far off,
you uninitiated ones.

Virgil

For the Luminous Woman in the Trees

Later, we would remember this
as one of the long days
at the end of the century,
those who would survive
their furies.
We walked out into the cemetery
to find a place to fuck
among the flowers of a fresh grave.
She wanted to eat the stars, she said,
but settled for me;
so hard for the newly dead
to make friends....
Evil, even in our kiss,
evil kiss, evil slaughter of lips.
Into rage we squandered our desire.
We hunched down in the wet grass
and hammered our hips together
exactly like dogs.

Elegy for the Swans
at Grace Pond

Bored with bread the children throw to her,
the swan who lost her one great love
when he washed up, tangled in the cold dawn,
drowned in the roots of the willow,
clings to the blue pond and its amnesia.
Grief makes her circle the willow's shadow
where she waits for him to reappear
evenings when the light disappears
and each lap of waves grows greener.
Before a hole opened up in the life
they'd invented in the clouds,
we watched them tangle their necks
around each other, sailing side by side
as to save themselves from our world.

The Offices of Loss

Before we warm our hands
enough to hold our books
the slow boy in the front
who never speaks begins
to cough then flies
out of his seat, twisted
into seizure. Because he's shocked
and gagging on his tongue
I should not stop to watch
the storm rage outside.
His gagging freezes the students
in their seats, scared deaf to my pleas
to find the nurse, shut off
the light and clear the bruising
desks away. When I reach him
through the flood of panicked air
he's stopped breathing, he's blue.
I can't pry loose his teeth
to drag his tongue back up
which like a fish eludes me
until I hook my finger
behind it, but still he's the pale
blue light of the drowned,
and someone's turned the lights
off so we collapse
between our worlds in the dark
swirling around us and I think
that he will die and I
drown into the trouble too
until he crosses back
and stares around the room
as if in another life

and we all strangers.
I'm always trapped between
things like that day
is why I have to tell this,
always of two minds,
singing the few songs
I know over and over,
their notes a gathering black
in the sky. An emptiness
does not abide in me.
An emptiness surrounds me.

This Man

There's another world, in which this man
dragged his prize beagle pup
off the aqua deep-pile carpet
where it had shit and pissed in excitement
when the children had wrongly
carried it in to play.

He never broke his stride.
He grabbed the pearl-handled pistol from the closet
and he dragged that pup who whined
into the backyard of an evening
in an autumn stuck somewhere, lost
in the currents of larger, less important things.

The Husband

Good morning is all we say to each other
in the morning, taking turns
trying to hurry the child
through his breakfast ritual of delay.
With two he is more difficult, as he
must try hard to divide himself for us
with our quiet demands. The grass is wet,
dew soaks my shoes on the way to the car.
A little dew on the shoes, a little
razor light streaking through our rented trees.

But I lose the morning and I'm trapped in less
gracious afternoon sun through the blinds of my
office and I remember her fingers
reflected in the window in the fallen
motel's café that night. Because we'd sinned
her fingers fidgeted on the table.
She tore the sugar wrapper into smaller
pieces, her hair like red dust rising
and words like sex in our mouths that night
we had high clouds in common, we had the harbor
beyond us of ships. We had the chance
for order and peace spread out like a picnic
in the green place, but words drown
and she's leaving and I'm holding her back,
tightening my fingers on her wrists,
tightening until the lines of what is permitted
and what is not
are no longer clear to us.

April

April and all the wrong you've done
with and to your life
begins to parade past you,

not like sheep, not so contented,
but like loud cars
and the gaudy Angel motorcycles,
over your bed and behind your eyes

so you get up and fill the house with light,
a signal to the dark neighborhood
which might think
that someone believes, or is afraid

and you put Coltrane on real low
(*More Lasting Than Bronze*)
and you lie down close to the box
and close your eyes....

The cadence keeps you sane.
The spacious forms give shape
to the everlasting music
that fills your brain—
not stress, but duration,
how the rain in April on these jonquils
lasts and lasts, luminous, enabling.

Autumn in the New Town

Each strange house among the dark trees has a light,
blue television glow crossed and recrossed
by mother waiting on father,
or the sewing at the night kitchen table,
or the repairs of small things whose survival
our own lives depend upon ridiculously,
God of the broken hovering over us.
In the trees a nightbird who must be
indigenous for the way he sings
a crazy morning song too loud for this hour
cuts some wing noise into the branches
and is gone into someone else's absent prayer,
and the bare branches rattle, Who are you
boy in the street
so precisely I turn around in a circle.
I wonder why my neighbors don't step out
when the bird sings so early.
I know he must be announcing something—
how it means so much to us
to hide and hold our fears in burning hearts,
but they must have gotten used to the bird,
like a corpse you must wash,
and it may be the shadows
cast across the streetlight's white cloth,
or the distance and its terrorists,
or a knot of nerves
growing wrong in my brain,
but I see them through their curtains
put on wings.

Meditation

Sprawled out in the warm sand, wine wise
and drowsy, we are carried off by the night
beyond the meter of waves,
the noise of things alive in the trees
persistent with their songs against
what they imagine threatens song,

you dream a world of voices we won't admit to
where the hungry spirits wear coats of longing,
the garden all splashed colors of trees
and birds and blue sky, the man and woman
not yet hiding themselves with their hands
and the snake curling in the tree behind them,

his long tongue calling to her, her hair
thrown back, the shape of her thighs and buttocks
as she reaches into the branches,
like an angel turning to flesh before him,
and then black space scarred
with the light of our grace burning out.

In the Autumn Village

Half in the street and half
up on the sidewalk
in the Village off of Eighth
a man in the Saturday cold air
without shoes
tried to crawl across the street
through busy traffic.
I'm no better than you,
but you've got to help a man
who's trying to go some place
on his hands and knees.
I don't know what it means to crawl,
or where you would go,
or in whose empty arms you could believe,

but I put my books down to help.
I offered my arm
as if to a girl
stepping from her father's porch
into an evening.
I thought he would pull himself
up on my arm
and walk away from us.
I was afraid, and bent over him
as if he might leap out at me.

I'm no goddamn better than you
but he couldn't move another inch
so I put my arms around him
and lifted him to the sidewalk.
The wind made some trees talk.
The city noise returned upon us,
a wave I could ride out on and away.

The Unattainable Body of Light

In the air, the sulfur smell of coal
from the furnace my father stoked
all winter long in a quietness
that grew around him like a cloak.
Smell of foundry in my face
when he picked me up
wildly over his head, smell of soap
on his neck when he held me,
his thick arms like snakes,
the whiskey on his lips like a wish.
Through the storm of years
there is no way back,
through all the bloody angles.

Why We Are Forgiven

Men still make steel in the hellish mill
though thousands are laid off and dazed
they do the shopping
for their working wives and dream
the blast furnace rumble.
Mill dust and red slag grit
is blood for some people.

Around hot steel these men twisted bands
until their fingers would not open in the morning,
and in my hungry brain
a spirit recalls my father,
home from the mill in his white T-shirt
like a god
and the smell of the mill

all over his body
and the taste of his delicious sweat.
Those evenings when he touched me,
those lingering hours after work and beer
when he reached down
into the nowhere my fear invented
I would come alive.

I would be drunk with joy
and in my small bed
I heard the ore boats
call from the river and the railcars

couple in the roundhouse
and the ringing hammer voices
of the night-shift workers sing us free.

May

I wanted to stay with my dog
when they did her in
I told the young veterinarian
who wasn't surprised.
Shivering on the chrome table,
she did not raise her eyes to me when I came in.
Something was resolved in her.
Some darkness exchanged for the pain.
There were a few more words
about the size of her tumor and her age,
and how we wanted to stop her suffering,
or our own, or stop all suffering
from happening before us
and then the nurse shaved May's skinny leg
with those black clippers;
she passed the needle to the doctor
and for once I knew what to do
and held her head against mine.
I cleaved to that smell
and lied into her ear
that it would be all right.
The veterinarian, whom I'd fought
about when to do this thing
said through tears
that it would take only a few minutes
as if that were not a long time
but there was no cry or growl,
only the weight of her in my arms,
and then on the world.

Anna's Grace

And with damp rags she bathes him,
brings him his whiskey in the evenings,
says the rosary before the crucifix
and dried palm leaves on the wall.
He can't stand by himself
or walk or lift his arms.
He doesn't know the children
or grandchildren who come to his bed
to hold his swollen hands
and kiss his face. On the plain
of stroke he sleeps in the day bed
where the sun may find him
and the toilet isn't far
when she must carry him
in to piss because he can't
hold his cock, so she holds it
for him, as when in love
they tumbled into the same bed.
He lies in the consuming
shock of the brain assaulting
itself and calls in the language
he would not abandon,
to the country dying out in his heart.
And the old woman who shaves him
with such grace he doesn't bleed,
sleeps on the hard couch,
flashlight on the table beside her
so she may shine and move
the light under her blankets
when he demands at night
to see no other man sleeps with her.

The Confusion of Planes
We Must Wander in Sleep

I stood naked in the corner as my mother
changed the wet sheet and clucked her tongue though spoke
as kindly as she could, my father stirring angrily
in the bed across the hall. Lost, my legs sheened in piss,
I stumbled, drugged with the grief
children practice to survive. I was apart
from the cold and heavy smell. I was not attached
to the world though I followed my young and weary
mother into the timeless dark, and tonight

I pull my own son's blankets back and speak to him:
how nice a dry bed will be, how good to get up
without a fuss and go. I lift him to stand,
his penis a wand waving its way magically
before us, and something makes sense for once in my head,
the way that what we pass on is not always a gift,
not always grace or strength or music, but sometimes
a burden, and we have no choice but to live
as hard as we can inside the storm of our years
because even the weaknesses are a kind of beauty
for the way they bind us into what love, finally, must be.

The Biography
of Fatty's Bar and Grille

Liquor was involved,
hard drinking all through the afternoon
and longtime bad blood
like a sickness,
and a woman who had dyed her hair
black as asphalt and whose breasts
swung freely inside her printed dress.
The man with three fingers kept a pistol
in the silk inner pocket
of his shark skin suit
and when the fat man
said one thing too many
to the woman under his breath
I heard that .22 pop three times
and watched the fat man
fall in a heap and grab his great belly.

Many people hit the floor,
though almost immediately
the shooter longed to bring the bullet back.
In disbelief he watched himself
convulse in fear and shame in the spidered mirror.
I remember how white his face became,
like a mask, like a spirit lost in its longing.
Then people began to rise up again.
Police and ambulance appeared.
The man with three fingers
was handcuffed with his arms before him
so when he smoked his cigarette
he looked like he was praying.

The Years
Without Understanding

My father did not read to me,
he would not quote anything or anyone,
he never alluded
as we are wont to say in my world
to poems or stories
to make a point or to teach me
some lesson about the life
beyond the slag heaps of our steel city
dying upon our dying lake.

And what you teach someone
with a belt across his back
is belts,
or I missed the point of those beatings
which were not so bad—
the loud voice in the hallway, then the belt
flashing
then the kisses on his lap.
If I could bring the words to you
as though from him,
clear as the air off this bay
you would see—

he is home from the foundry,
younger than I am now, the black
dust from the mill like a mask
and he is bending down to me
in the dusk where I've waited

on the steps of the bar
for his bus
and the cathedral
he makes with his fingers
opens to a silver dime
he twists before me
and lays down into my hands
for being good he says.

Meditation at Pearl Street

In the steelyard, long line of workers
changing shifts, hunched in the predawn cold,
caught in light from mill towers like
search lights. And the gas flaming up
blue and white from the open hearth
that blasted ingots of iron and carbon into steel.
And the beauty of our slag heaps,
black desert by the lake where we met
in secret as boys to smoke and to touch
ourselves, our legs stiffening, the gull's cry
an accusation. And the small company houses
painted in pastels against the fly ash
that came down on us like dogwood dust....
Into what grief,
into what family of grief were we born
and did we grow
that these things are grace.
In the quiet hours,
when the chronic angers were still
and the father's curses
did not slam down on the table
a rough love bound us in a feast
where all our hearts were opened.

The Black Hose

A boy who knew enough to save for something
like the whim that took me downtown on the bus
one lost Saturday, morning of my mother's birthday,
I sat in the back where the gasoline smell
made me dizzy and I closed my eyes but didn't
think of her, only of myself, basking in the light
and love that would fall down on me when I
handed her the box and she untied the bow to save
and lifted something shining out and held it up before us
like a promise taking shape for once in her hands,
though I didn't know what to buy, the bus door
hissing behind me because I'm in some kind of
state now, a trance that comes when you pull
at the cords of light that connect the mother to the boy,
the 1959 department store
opening up before me like a jeweled city.
In lingerie I found myself
surrounded by those torsos sheened in silk,
dreaming my mother, feeling the silk against me,
the two of us moving through a cloudy room
in a dance I can't remember until shame comes.
From out of nowhere the matron frowned,
asked what I wanted, hovered over me.
Confused and afraid I whispered, without thinking,
The black hose with rhinestones down the seams please
and pointed to the pair across the room
stretched over legs on the glass counter
as if about to step off
and I saw her in my mind slip them on,
her skirt hiked above the garters, the sun

catching in her tangled hair
until the matron made a sound in her throat
and looked at me with eyes that said
What's wrong with you dirty boy.

All the way home a sweet ache rocked me,
the silver package riding my lap
like a heavy wrong thing
I couldn't give up no matter how it
dragged me down to a place
where I could barely breathe or see or feel.
Whatever happened that spinning afternoon—
she ran her fingers over the rhinestone seams
or she didn't, she wore them out into an evening
or kept them forever in her drawer of impossible things—
doesn't matter. I would find my way into the light
of another woman into whose arms I fall
nights my fingers can't tear through the dark
that eats me, the silk stretched across her breasts,
the need for something womanly to raise me up
pounding in my head until I curl in sleep
away from those longings, ancient and blue.

The Third Person

How peculiar the birds in the ivy,
how strange they seem to him,
like faces in the ivy of women
from another far life,
so he wonders
what jungle can keep its promises.
On the phone he says
The walls are closing in
because he cannot imagine
his voice stretching across the long wire.
The walls are closing in....
What a sentimental guy,
what a killing guy,

and in his loss of hours,
in his room of years
he pictures the mill stacks of home
and the open-hearth's glow
on the street of filthy bars
where the fathers walked
from one century into the next
in black fly ash masks of despair.

Outside on the window ledge
pigeons huddle and pester.
From his room he sees them as clearly
as his sins or his lies.
They stretch their oily wings
and coo through the frozen window
in wisps of escaping heat.
Someone drags their fingers
through him and is gone.

Blues at the Equinox

In the shadows
the woman dresses quietly,
beyond light the parking lot

spears through thin drapes,
her heart inclined
towards the miraculous.

What passes for love,
the miles and the years
and the rivers crossed no one could name,

what passes for love
is not always the fierce blessing
the mortal lovers give—and then grow pale—

but sometimes one heart robbing another
in a rented room, a great sadness
and a great happiness, at the same time, descending.

The Impossible

Winter's last rain and a light I don't recognize
through the trees and I come back in my mind
to the man who made me suck his cock
when I was seven, in sunlight, between boxcars.
I thought I could leave him standing there
in the years, half smile on his lips,
small hands curled into small fists,
but after he finished, he held my hand in his
as if astonished, until the houses were visible
just beyond the railyard. He held my hand
but before that he slapped me hard on the face
when I would not open my mouth for him.

I do not want to say his whole hips
slammed into me, but they did, and a black wave
washed over my brain, changing me
so I could not move among my people in the old way.
On my way home I stopped in the churchyard
to try and find a way to stay alive.
In the branches a redwing flitted, warning me.
In the rectory, Father prepared
the body and blood for mass
but God could not save me from a mouthful of cum.
That afternoon some lives turned away from the light.
He taught me how to move my tongue around.
In his hands he held my head like a lover.
Say it clearly and you make it beautiful, no matter what.

The Forms
of Eleventh Avenue

I squatted like I'd learned in Dak To
on the seventh floor window ledge
across from the park of the homeless
contemplating the skyline and the loss.
In milky light behind me
the woman who would be exiled
slept, her feet moving
like a dog's in a dream.
Men smoked glass pipes
in the streetlight's
wash across the park.
Women tried to nurture
into existence
homes from cardboard boxes.
Four policemen talked
and snapped their sticks
on a park bench.
All night on the ledge
spirits called to me:
Come to us with your face
and your wings
they whispered
from their saintly streets
and the human things
could not save me.
Not the smell
of the woman's hair
in the morning
like street air after rain.
Not the corpses
waking in doorways.

Not the way everything changes,
continuously, like the sky.
What saved me
were the Latin prayers
come back from the years
like desire,
and the many mouths
open in absolution,
and the nakedness,
the belt flashing,
the fists from out of nowhere,
the abandonment of love.

Notes

"What Saves Us" is for Sally.

"They Name Heaven" was written in memory of Tomás Rivera.

"The Sky in Daduza Township" is based on a photograph by Paul Weinberg (Afrapix), which appeared originally in *TriQuarterly* #69 (Spring/Summer 1987). The poem is dedicated to Reg Gibbons.

The title "The Hand That Takes" is inspired by Laurie Anderson's song "O Superman."

"Meditation" is for Dave Smith, and was inspired by his tidewater poems.

"Meditation at Pearl Street" is for Gloria Emerson who suggested the Lorain poems. The final two lines are a variation on lines from Pablo Neruda.

The line "what a killing guy" in "The Third Person" is based on a phrase from Dos Passos.

The lines "is not always the fierce blessing / the mortal lovers give—and then grow pale— " in "Blues at the Equinox" are a variation on lines from John Keats.

"The Impossible" is for Toby Thompson.

☆

Bruce Weigl is the author of six collections of poetry, most recently *Song of Napalm*. His poetry, essays, articles and reviews have appeared in such magazines and journals as the *Nation*, *TriQuarterly*, *American Poetry Review*, *Paris Review* and *Harper's*. Weigl has been awarded the Pushcart Prize, fellowships at Breadloaf and YADDO, and a grant from the National Endowment for the Arts. He teaches in the writing program at The Pennsylvania State University and is past president of the Associated Writing Programs.